Link to the Past,
Bridge to the Future

Link to the Past, Bridge to the Future

Colonial Williamsburg's Animals

by John P. Hunter

Photography by David M. Doody
Additional photography by Tom Green, Barbara Lombardi,
Kelly Mihalcoe, and Lael White

Colonial Williamsburg
The Colonial Williamsburg Foundation
Williamsburg, Virginia

16 15 14 13 12 11 10 09 08 07 06 05   1 2 3 4 5 6 7 8 9 10

Printed in Singapore

Library of Congress Cataloging-in-Publication Data

Hunter, John P.
  Link to the past, bridge to the future : Colonial Williamsburg's animals / by John P. Hunter.
     p. cm.
  Includes bibliographical references (p.   ).
  ISBN-13: 978-0-87935-193-9 (alk. paper) 1. Rare breeds—Virginia—Williamsburg—History.
2. Livestock breeds—Virginia—Williamsburg—History. 3. Zoology, Economic—Virginia—
Williamsburg. I. Title.
  SF105.275.U6H86 2005
  636.08'2'097554252—dc22

ISBN-13: 978-0-87935-193-9   2005019977
ISBN-10: 0-87935-193-4

Designed by Helen M. Olds

Original photography directed by Abigail Schumann

*Colonial Williamsburg is a registered trade name of
The Colonial Williamsburg Foundation, a not-for-profit
educational institution.*

The Colonial Williamsburg Foundation
PO Box 1776
Williamsburg, VA 23187-1776
www.colonialwilliamsburg.org

President's Message

THE COLONIAL WILLIAMSBURG FOUNDATION IS FORTUNATE to have many friends who believe profoundly in our work. Three enthusiastic donors in particular have taken a special interest in our Rare Breeds program and have made possible the publication of this book. We are grateful to Mr. and Mrs. Donald H. Wagoner of New York City and Ms. Estelle Walgreen of Lake Forest, Illinois, for their generous support.

Karen and Donald Wagoner have been friends of the Foundation for over twenty-five years. They have lived all over the world, yet they have never lost touch with Colonial Williamsburg. They have a deep appreciation for endangered animals and have been interested in Colonial Williamsburg's Rare Breeds program since its inception. They hope that this book helps to educate and inspire others.

Estelle Walgreen has a particular love of animals. She raises pot-bellied pigs among many other animals at home and on her farm in West Virginia. Her personal knowledge of animal husbandry has led her to explore this most interesting aspect of Colonial Williamsburg's intensive study of colonial life and culture. Like the Wagoners, Ms. Walgreen has a deep regard for education and believes the publication of this book will bring greater attention to an important subject in an accessible format that should appeal to a broad audience.

I am pleased to formally thank Mr. and Mrs. Wagoner and Ms. Walgreen. Their gifts enable us to share the stories of Colonial Williamsburg's animals, which are a vital part of our mission—*That the future may learn from the past.*

Colin G. Campbell
The Colonial Williamsburg Foundation

FOREWORD

THE COLONIAL WILLIAMSBURG FOUNDATION exhibits the world's largest living history museum. Through its environs, people, and programs, it re-creates and interprets life as it was in the eighteenth-century capital of the colony of Virginia. As part of this effort, the Foundation has an extensive livestock program to help support its mission: "That the future may learn from the past."

This book illustrates some of the situations where livestock would have been used in those earlier times. It opens a window into our past through images that conjure up the vital interactions between the inhabitants and the animals that shared their daily lives.

How different life was then from our modern lives. Most people in the colonies lived a rural life and livestock was a natural part of daily living. Today, the majority of the population live in urban settings. The closest most people come to livestock on a daily basis is at the meat counter in the grocery store.

The change in agriculture to feed an ever-increasing population has made vast differences in the way we produce food and raise livestock. It has also produced many changes in the breeds of animals raised.

Livestock breeds have become more specialized, and the number of different breeds in a species is continually being reduced due to the dominance of one or two breeds. In milk cows, for example, the Holstein dominates the industry due to its high milk-production rate. As a result, many of the breeds that produce less milk have dwindled in numbers. These breeds have become rare and even extinct. There are many such examples throughout the livestock world.

These rare breeds are often the older breeds developed over the past centuries by farmers throughout the world to suit their specific circumstances. An animal's adaptability to a particular environment and regional livestock practices produced unique varieties. When we lose them, we lose not only the breeds and their distinctive genetic makeup but also a link to our past.

Colonial Williamsburg's livestock program strives to maintain some of these rarer breeds and their unique genetic makeups through the Rare Breeds program. Many of the breeds of livestock in this program are similar to the kinds of livestock found in Virginia in the eighteenth century and thus allow us to create a more complete picture of life as it was then.

Richard Nicoll
Director, Coach and Livestock Department
The Colonial Williamsburg Foundation

GEORGE WASHINGTON, THOMAS JEFFERSON, AND PATRICK HENRY would have found it most unusual to walk the streets of eighteenth-century Williamsburg and not encounter horses, oxen, poultry, cats, dogs, and cows. As the capital and major social and commercial center of the colony of Virginia, Williamsburg offered the town's residents and visitors high society, high finance, central government, and a pungent sensory experience. Animals were a big part of the bustling scene, and the sounds of livestock were a constant background chorus.

The importance of animals in the eighteenth century cannot be overstated. Every one of the Founding Fathers used horses for work, pleasure, and transportation. Most raised cattle, and many owned sheep. It is almost certain that they all kept some type of poultry. Regardless of one's station in society, however, interactions with livestock were commonplace. In the country and the city, animals were an integral part of daily life for literally everyone.

In Colonial Williamsburg's Historic Area, the meticulously restored capital of colonial-era Virginia, the presence of livestock continues to enhance an understanding of the day-to-day realities of colonial life. There is something timelessly reassuring about sheep in a pasture or the clop-clop of horses' hooves as they pull a coach down Duke of Gloucester Street. We simply connect to animals, and the link has been there throughout the ages. In our modern turbo-techno world, daily survival may not hinge as precariously on the backs of animals as it once did, but, then again, maybe it does.

Colonial Williamsburg began its Rare Breeds program in 1986 to preserve genetic diversity in livestock and to showcase animals in the Historic Area that are similar to those that lived in and around colonial-era Williamsburg. By successfully breeding these rare animals, Colonial Williamsburg prevents the loss of

breeds important to the history and development of American farming livestock. The program complements Colonial Williamsburg's living history interpretation by portraying another aspect of daily life in colonial Virginia.

The Rare Breeds program's road from concept to practical application requires specialized technical skills and fosters many day-to-day challenges for the Coach and Livestock Department. Whether employing sophisticated artificial insemination techniques or the natural alternative, suitable parents must first be located, traded, bought, or borrowed. Animal pregnancies and births can be easy or difficult, but every step is monitored. Tracking and registration paperwork abounds. Educational and promotional aspects of the program are bolstered by electronic field trips, consumer products, press and photo opportunities. Creative livestock programs of interest to all ages are designed to stir and sustain present and future interest.

The coordinated effort pays off for all the Historic Area animals and their audiences. Healthy, well-kept horses pulling carriages down Historic Area streets delight Colonial Williamsburg guests. Varieties of poultry in the chicken yards entertain with their nonstop busy work. In the spring, energetic lambs cavort in the small pastures throughout the town.

Not often visible is the effort behind the effect. Like almost anything worthwhile, the tasks are neither predictable nor easy. Guests miss the scramble to bring in an alternate team of horses from an outlying pasture when one of the scheduled work horses turns up lame. They might never see the lamb being bottle-fed every two hours because its mother isn't producing any milk or the nightly slathering of petroleum jelly onto the legs of a rooster with a scale infection. Numerous pastures and poultry yards throughout the Historic Area must be visited twice every day. Among many other duties, the sheep and poultry are counted and the numbers recorded, feed is delivered, and any necessary medical care is administered.

The Coach and Livestock Department staff meet these challenges on a regular basis. Whether in the form of a lame horse, a ewe lambing three weeks early, or a dairy cow with mastitis, the one thing that can be planned for when working with animals is that something unplanned will happen every day. Coach and Livestock tasks and responsibilities play out 365 days a year.

Public interpretations not only instruct guests on the prevalence of livestock in colonial life but also introduce the concepts and goals behind Colonial Williamsburg's breed preservation efforts. The program seems more relevant with each passing year.

Preserving historical breeds might well have ramifications far beyond providing a realistic colonial backdrop for field trip or family photos. A passion for the future shapes the Coach and Livestock's Rare Breeds program as significantly as linkage to the past. In this contemporary world where many corporate providers raise livestock in close quarters on enhanced feed, the simplicity of grazing on grass in an open field might one day contribute as much to humanity as it does to the general well-being of the animals.

After decades of selective breeding, chemical enhancement, and stagnant environs, many present-day food animals are simply dependent on that combination to survive. As can happen when there is no diversity, immune systems weaken, physiological characteristics stagnate, and end products become predictable if not bland. Production levels become difficult to maintain unless all conditions are perfect. There has to be import given to the fact that a breed no longer in fashionable or commercially viable vogue and raised unfettered on grass is healthier and more resistant to disease and degeneration. These animals also, well, taste better on the dinner plate. We may not know exactly how the characteristics these rare breeds possess might one day save our bacon and beef and scrambled eggs and warm wool topcoats, but it is a bank account we cannot afford to close.

The program began with some red cows.

ON AUGUST 31, 1775, AN ADVERTISEMENT in the *Virginia Gazette* listed a "red cow and calf" and a "red steer" among animals missing from a plantation in Hanover County. The animals could well have been Devon cattle, a versatile breed that produced milk for calves and dairy products and beef for consumption and had great strength as draft animals. The first Devons arrived in Massachusetts from England in 1623.

Many cows, very likely including Devons, were kept in Williamsburg proper to supply milk, cream, and other dairy products to their respective households. They were often simply called "town cows," and the convenience they provided their owners balanced out the inconvenience of having to quarter them in the restricted confines of the town. Other than on market days, steers raised for beef were rarely housed inside the city. Of course, the country was only a few hundred yards in any direction.

Long-held beliefs about the historic Chesapeake diet, specifically that colonials ate more pork than beef, are changing. Archaeology and individual colonial household accounts are shedding new light on meat consumption. Surprisingly, the conclusion reached is that more beef than pork was consumed by colonial Virginians. Poor rural free men and slaves may have eaten proportionally more pork than did the more well-to-do, but, on every site, the percentage of beef surpasses that of pork. Devon cuts were surely part of the colonial meat-for-consumption mix.

Out on the farms, Devon oxen exhibited great strength, an even pace, a willingness to work, and the ability to endure extremes of climate. Nineteenth-century authorities on livestock such as William Youatt and William Housman praised the Devon as a draft animal. Amazingly, these mahogany-colored cattle, originating in Devonshire, England, were not selectively bred by man to achieve their particular traits.

Even cattle hair helped build Williamsburg. In the eighteenth century, plaster was made of lime, sand, and animal hair, usually from cattle, horses, goats, or pigs. Animal hair was a superior binder and added greatly to the structural integrity of many a colonial wall. Today, the mixture continues to produce an excellent plaster. Colonial Williamsburg brickmakers used authentic cattle-hair plaster in the Historic Area

to recoat the interior walls of the Peyton Randolph Dairy; the Benjamin Powell Dairy, an original building; and the George Davenport Stable, also referred to as the Presbyterian Meetinghouse. The brickmakers give assurance that, even if the plaster should crack, it will hold together thanks to the cattle hair in the mix.

Specialization and mechanization, the twin prongs of progress, nearly pushed Devon cattle into extinction. Devons could not compete with Holsteins and Jerseys in the arena of milk production. Mechanical farm equipment virtually eliminated the use of oxen as working animals in the ever more industrialized world. As the years passed and developing specific function became the trend in breeding practices, the Devon was subdivided through selective breeding into separate lines of beef cattle and dairy animals. The dairy line became known as the Milking Devon.

By the 1970s, fewer than one hundred Milking Devons remained in the United States, and the breed was extinct in England. Still, all indications were that Devon cattle are authentic to colonial-era Williamsburg, and Devons were what the Rare Breeds program wanted on the property again.

Milking Shorthorns

Milking Devons

In 1986, the Rare Breeds program made its first acquisition, a Milking Devon cow named Nora. Breeding efforts have been successful, and the project has helped breathe new life into the future of the Devon. Each year Colonial Williamsburg adds five to nine calves to the Devon population. Approximately thirteen Devons are kept on-site. In addition, Colonial Williamsburg keeps four Milking Shorthorns to help with the work in the Historic Area. The Milking Shorthorn, often referred to as the Durham, is also a rare breed and authentic to the eighteenth century.

To produce milk, a cow must first produce a calf. Milk production, biologically speaking, is a supply-and-demand process: the greater the demand, the more abundant the supply, within certain parameters. This balance is nature's way of ensuring that a growing calf gets sufficient nourishment. When necessary and if

she has ample milk, a cow can be milked once a day while her calf is still nursing.

More commonly, regular milking takes place after the calf has been weaned. Calves begin to wean naturally at about three to four months of age. Milking twice a day, every day, at the same time of day, keeps the milk flowing and the cow healthy. Depending on the breed, a cow's body will continue to respond to the demand for milk for five to ten months after the calf is weaned. After that period, her production ceases. To make more milk, the cow must be bred again and produce another calf.

Milking cows and the subsequent dairying was time-consuming work in the eighteenth century. It was also women's work. In fact, it wasn't until the mechanization and commercialization of dairy operations in the nineteenth and early twentieth centuries that men became extensively involved in this age-old process.

Then as now, milking a single cow by hand could take as little as ten minutes or as long as half an hour. The duration of the task depended on the speed and skill of the dairymaid, the amount of milk available, and the cooperation of the cow. If uncooperative, a cow can actually hold up her milk, or deliver an attention-getting kick. A cow's udder is divided into four quarters, and each quarter must

be milked out individually. It is important to remove all the milk in the udder: the resulting void creates the physiological demand that keeps the cow in full milk production.

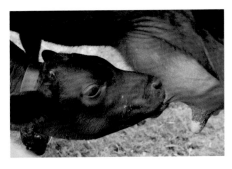

In colonial times, milking was often the first chore in the morning and the final major chore of the day. Today, Coach and Livestock staff members milk once a day. A nursing calf handles the second milking. It is important that the animal be milked at the same time each day. Otherwise, the pressure in the cow's udder from a buildup of milk can become quite uncomfortable after several hours. An erratic milking schedule can cause milk production to drop or, worse, lead to a painful and potentially harmful infection of the udder called *mastitis*. Twelve hours between each milking was and continues to be the ideal, but, even in the eighteenth century, a heavy milking cow could be milked up to three times a day.

The Coach and Livestock staff offers milking demonstrations in the Historic Area seasonally. The demonstrations provide a forum for staff to discuss the importance of multipurpose cattle in the eighteenth century and for guests to see the cattle up close and ask questions.

But dairy work only begins with milking. To have cream, butter, and cheese, there is additional work to be done. When fresh milk is poured into deep, wide bowls and left to sit several hours, the cream separates from the milk and rises to the top. In a colonial household, the cream was then skimmed off the milk and stored in cream pots or churned into butter.

Churning butter was and is one of life's simple mysteries. In the eighteenth century, churning was accomplished with a plunge churn. The agitation by the plunger causes the solids that comprise the cream to congeal. The congealing forces out the remaining liquid, or *buttermilk* (which is not the same as the cultured buttermilk you can buy at the grocery store), and produces a firm mass of butter. Depending on the butterfat content of the milk, it takes about ten quarts of cow's milk to get enough cream to make a pound of butter. Conveniently, Devon milk is high in butterfat content. Still, in a typical colonial household, it could have taken a week or more of skimming milk to collect enough cream to make butter.

Whereas butter is made from fat, cheese involves the proteins in milk. Thus, making cheese starts with the milk. An enzyme called *rennet* is added to cause the protein solids in the milk to congeal. Rennet comes from the stomachs of young milk-fed mammals, like calves. The congealed solids are the curds; the liquid is the whey. The whey is drained off, leaving a soft cheese of tightly formed curds. While today's cheese makers take additional steps to produce an endless variety of cheeses, this simple process produces a soft farmer cheese that was common table fare in the Revolutionary period and is quite compatible with modern-day tastes as well. It takes about four and a half quarts of milk to make one pound of cheese.

These same products are made today by Colonial Williamsburg's Foodways program, which receives the rich, fresh milk from the daily milkings to make butter, soft cheeses, puddings, and milk-based beverages. Interpreters with the Foodways program research recipes, ingredients, and cooking processes from the colonial era and incorporate them into an active hearth cooking program in Historic Area kitchens. As they prepare and cook, they teach guests about colonial food processing, cooking, and consumption.

Overall, dairy products did not fare well in the colonial dog days of summer unless they were consumed shortly after leaving the cow. But, as cooler temperatures came on, cream, butter, and soft cheeses gained an extended shelf life.

Because of careful selection and breeding, the Milking Devon cattle seen in Colonial Williamsburg's pastures could well be the closest in America to the Devons originally imported to Massachusetts in the 1600s. Each year, new calves preserve that original genetic diversity and are a visible testimony to the success of the Rare Breeds program.

THE DEVONS BROUGHT AN AUTHENTIC reddish hue to the Historic Area palette, but the woolen white of period ewes, rams, and lambs was missing. There are many successful, healthy breeds of sheep throughout the world, but just having sheep around was not good enough for the Rare Breeds program. Foundation research showed that the Leicester Longwool was one sheep breed that could have grazed in the fields around colonial-era Williamsburg. Identifying a sheep with the right lineage and a fascinating history was one thing. Finding one turned out to be quite another.

In the eighteenth century, the Leicester (pronounced "Lester") was a groundbreaking, scientifically significant animal. The breed was introduced to the world by eighteenth-century gentleman farmer Robert Bakewell of Leicestershire, England. He was among the first to successfully select specific genetic traits in livestock that breed true, consistently producing offspring with the same genetic characteristics as their parents.

The result of Bakewell's efforts, the Leicester, became known as the "barrel on four short legs." Bakewell bred the Leicester Longwool sheep as a dual-purpose animal to produce ample wool and abundant, quality meat, and the animal set a high standard. Maturing faster than other breeds, it fulfilled Bakewell's desire to give England "two pounds of mutton where there was only one before."

Colonial planters also were interested in increasing the quality of their livestock. In 1792, George Washington wrote to a fellow farmer, Henry Dorsey Gough: "I had paid much attention to my Sheep, and was proud in being able to produce perhaps the largest mutton and the greatest quantity of Wool from my Sheep that could be then produced. But I was not satisfied with this, and contemplated further improvements both in the flesh and wool by the introduction of other breeds, which I should by this time have carried into effect, had I been permitted to pursue my favorite occupation." Washington, along with fellow planters, was well aware and appreciative of Bakewell's work. Washington noted in a letter to his overseer in 1793 that Bakewell's breeding practices would very likely improve the health and production of his flock.

Leicester Longwools

Based on the inherent authenticity of the Leicester sheep to the setting, Colonial Williamsburg was anxious to have the animals in evidence. However, due to market changes, among other reasons, pure Leicester Longwool sheep were extinct in the United States by the early 1900s. The hunt was on. Eventually, a ram lamb from a small Canadian flock was found and purchased at a New Jersey auction.

Willoughby arrived in Williamsburg in 1985. While the Foundation searched for Leicester ewes, Willoughby was bred to Dorset ewes, a very old breed that had been in evidence in colonial times. Beautiful crossbred lambs were produced by this cozy arrangement up until 1988 when Willoughby was tragically killed.

The quest for a flock of Leicesters intensified. After an international search, Ivan Heazlewood, a third-generation Leicester breeder in Tasmania, got involved. He personally took on the considerable task of organizing a flock of sheep for export to Williamsburg. He began by selecting ewes from four different flocks and arranging to have them bred to rams that remained behind in Tasmania. He selected a ram and included several ewes from his own flock in the group intended for Colonial Williamsburg. After clearing all the standard health inspections in Australia,

the sheep arrived in Canada for a quarantine period and the final leg of their trip. In February 1990, after many long and anxious months, eight beautiful Leicester Longwool ewes, six lambs, and one ram arrived in Williamsburg.

Dr. Phil S. Sponenberg, technical advisor for the American Livestock Breeds Conservancy, an organization dedicated to monitoring and promoting vanishing farm animal breeds, designed a breeding plan for Colonial Williamsburg. The goal was to make the most of the genetic material available and to avoid inbreeding and other pitfalls of working with a small population of sheep. Following two successful breeding seasons, Colonial Williamsburg began establishing healthy satellite flocks by loaning sheep to other breeders in the United States.

Like colonial shepherds, the present-day Coach and Livestock husbandry staff is busy in the springtime. In early spring, the staff is on around-the-clock "lamb watch" as the ewes near their due dates for giving birth. Each birth is an important event in the continuing viability of the Rare Breeds program. Extensive records are kept for each sheep. The animal's lineage is tracked, recorded, and registered. Each lamb's weight is documented along with any unusual or notable pregnancy or delivery problems experienced by the ewe. General health records note medications, aliments, and procedures for each individual animal. Additionally, the length, texture, and quality of each sheep's fleece is charted and retained.

Late spring brings the task of shearing. In 1765, John Wily wrote in his *Treatise on the Propagation of Sheep,* "The proper Time to shear your Sheep is in the Increase of the Moon, in *May*."

A small farmer living on the outskirts of Williamsburg might have enlisted his entire household in the shearing of the flock. Confining the animals in a sheepfold, or pen, allowed for ease of selection. Depending on the size of the flock, it might have taken one day or several to shear all the sheep, trim their hooves, and administer any necessary medications. Like all grazing animals, sheep are prone to intestinal worms. Tobacco juice or mercury-based purges were used to expel these debilitating parasites.

Although many sheep were shorn "in the dirt," meaning that they were not washed beforehand, it was not uncommon, when convenient, to wash the entire flock several days before shearing. Convenience was dictated by whether there was a pond, stream, or river nearby deep enough to soak the sheep. Dirt and grime come away from the wool with gentle agitation since most of the dirt is on the surface. Sheep produce a grease called *lanolin* that serves as a lubricant for the sheep's wool and aids in repelling water. Lanolin traps dirt on the outer layers of the fleece while underneath the wool remains clean.

Today, Coach and Livestock interpreters offer shearing-by-hand demonstrations that faithfully mimic the methods used in colonial times. The sheep shearer begins by first turning the sheep onto its back or, more precisely, its haunches. This maneuver is easier than it sounds. Curiously, once sheep are off their feet, more often than not, they just lie there. This behavior might be attributable to the fact that sheep are prey animals. They have little in the way of defense mechanisms other than to run away. When this option is removed, instinct may be instructing them to keep still and avoid drawing attention to themselves. Whatever the cause, this passive response to being upended works to the advantage of the shearer.

A fleece is shorn in a prescribed pattern beginning with the chest and belly wool. This is the lowest quality wool on the sheep and is generally discarded or used as padding and stuffing. The prime wool is along the sides of the sheep. If a colonial-era sheep was to be sold or auctioned after shearing, one lock of wool, called a *buyer's lock,* was left unshorn to show prospective buyers the length of a full fleece on the animal.

A well-shorn fleece comes away intact, held together by miniscule interlocking fibers between the strands of wool. John Wily continued in his *Treatise on the Propagation of Sheep*, "It will be proper the Person employed to shear the Sheep should carefully roll up each Fleece by itself, turning it inside out."

Frequently, hand spinners are among the interested spectators at Colonial Williamsburg's shearing demonstrations. Leicester fleece is very desirable for this craft, which is rapidly growing in popularity today. In colonial days, spinning was certainly more than a hobby. According to a study of York County estate inventories of middling planters, 80 percent owned spinning wheels, which were used to spin wool into yarn, and 24 percent had looms and could turn yarn into cloth. The yarn and cloth were, most likely, for home use but may also have supplemented a middling planter's income.

Eighteenth-century Williamsburg estate inventories for only two town dwellers list sheep, yet their presence on farms surrounding the capital is clear. In 1765, Williamsburg printer Joseph Royal published a treatise on the propagation of sheep in Virginia. And in 1769 and 1770, associations of Virginia House of Burgesses members and leading Williamsburg merchants signed agreements restricting the importation of goods from England and encouraging the raising of sheep for the benefit of the colony. George Washington had strong feelings on the subject, as he expressed in a 1792 letter to Henry Dorsey Gough: "I have ever been satisfied in my own mind, that by a proper attention to our Sheep . . . they might be made not only a most profitable subject to the farmer, but rendered highly important in a public view."

William Youatt, the early nineteenth-century British veterinarian, observed in his book on sheep breeds and diseases that the new Leicesters "within little more than half a century spread themselves from their native county over every part of the United Kingdom, and are now exported in great number to the continents of Europe and America."

It is amazing that in the relatively short time since Youatt made those comments, the Leicester essentially vanished, a consequence of the darker side of progress. Luckily, there are those who appreciate the value of distinctive breed characteristics and are dedicated to their preservation. Today, the Leicester Longwool is a success story. Thanks in great part to the Colonial Williamsburg Rare Breeds program, the breed has a much healthier and prolific outlook.

Since its official establishment in the Historic Area in 1990, the Leicester Longwool continues to be a favorite with guests. To initiate and sustain the interest of children in rare breeds, a Leicester lamb is actually given to a young person each year. The recipient is chosen based on an essay. That child, who must have facilities conducive to the task, is responsible for raising the lamb and eventually making good use of the animal, such as using the fleece to make wool products.

Like the multitasking Devon cattle that along with their leather and labor supplied milk and beef for the table, so too did the Leicester sheep contribute to the pots and plates of colonial-era Virginia. Mutton and lamb helped satisfy the enormous colonial appetite for meat, but it could be expensive.

Ossabaw Island pigs

ENTER THE PIGS. PORK WAS AN EXTREMELY well-liked alternative to the expensive beef, mutton, and lamb. Because they were a cheap source of meat, hogs were very popular in colonial Virginia. The animals reproduce rapidly and are easily fattened, and their meat preserves very well. In addition, hogs thrive with almost no supervision and a flexible food supply.

Pigs were brought to Virginia from England and perhaps, according to the following account, from Bermuda. In 1609, under the command of Adm. George Somers, the ship *Sea Venture* set sail from England with supplies and settlers for the two-year-old Jamestown colony. After seven weeks at sea, the ship encountered a fierce storm and eventually sank on the coral reefs of Bermuda. The passengers, crew, and ship's dog made it safely to the island. A large hog soon wandered into camp, presumably descended from those left by some previous shipwreck. The hog was oblivious to the danger and easily captured. The castaways built pens for the wild pigs and fed them with the abundant berries from palmetto trees. Rescue and grand adventure in island-made boats may have resulted in some of these Bermuda pigs being brought to Jamestown.

Pigs quickly thrived in the colonies. Pork products became standard items on Virginia's dining tables as well as exports to New England and, subsequently, to British sugar plantations in the West Indies and on to Great Britain.

Today, Colonial Williamsburg guests can witness a colonial era–inspired butchering demonstration by the Foundation's Foodways program in early December. Interpreters use period tools and procedures in the process. The meat is very fatty, not appealing to today's consumers.

These swine are Ossabaw Island pigs, a unique breed left on one of Georgia's barrier islands by Spanish explorers in the sixteenth century. Interestingly, the Ossabaw Island pigs, with their fatty meat, may one day leave their most significant legacy to science not cuisine. Unlike other breeds of swine, Ossabaw Island pigs share a common trait with humans: having had to adapt to a feast or famine existence in the extreme environment of the isolated island, the Ossabaw Island pigs developed a genetic predisposition to obesity. For both the

pigs and humans, this adaptation is a mechanism to survive famine. In today's world of plentiful food and minimal exercise, however, this characteristic is leading to diabetes and heart disease in humans. The pigs, though, under their natural active conditions, keep this predisposition to obesity under control and remain healthy. Through continuing studies of the pigs, researchers hope to reveal useful information in the quest for human diabetes and heart disease relief and eventual cure.

Although Ossabaw Island pork is a little fatty for modern tastes, similar pigs were a hit in colonial Virginia. Hogs in the early 1600s would have been left loose in the woods to forage food for themselves, being penned only to fatten for slaughter. Folk lore attributes the delicious unique taste of colonial Virginia's hams to a diet of snakes. Snakes or not, the nonfinicky hogs for sure dined on insects and nuts that accumulated on the ground.

In 1688, parson John Clayton wrote to the Royal Society of London that Virginia ham was "I believe as good as any *Westphalia* [a German duchy then famous for the finest hams in Europe], certainly far exceeding our *English*." According to the good reverend, who shared an interest in the natural world with the English bishop who sent him to Jamestown in 1684, the secret of this superlative flavor was not due to just the pigs' diet. He observed that the meat-curing process involving salting, smoking, and aging did much to distinguish the unique flavor of Virginia hams.

Salt-curing provided colonists with a way to preserve meat without refrigeration; the smoking process added flavor and aroma. Due to the lack of refrigeration, a cold month, often December, was the logical time for the butchering, salting, and smoking of colonial pigs. Fundamentally, there were two steps in the curing process. The hams and sides of bacon were first rubbed well with

coarse salt, packed into tubs of salt, and left for six weeks. The salt drew out the water from the meat. For the next one to two weeks, the salted meats were exposed to a smoldering fire that burned in a tightly constructed wooden or brick shed. After aging in the same smokehouse for up to two years, dried, long-lasting, smoke-flavored meat was ready for consumption.

Colonial Williamsburg carries on the tradition, beginning with the salting of the pork in December. After remaining in the salting tubs for six weeks, the cuts are hung over the smokehouse fire. Green wood is used because the objective is to make smoke, not flame. Historically, some Virginians used corncobs or fruitwood, which also provided adequate smoke for the task. Apple wood added a certain sweetness to the meat smoked at Shirley Plantation in Charles City County, Virginia.

A smokehouse was a necessity for practically every household in colonial times. They were numerous then, and, today, twelve of Colonial Williamsburg's eighty-eight surviving original structures are smokehouses. In his work on life in America in the 1790s, Thomas Cooper, an English-born lawyer, scientist, and philosopher, described in detail how smokehouses were made and used: "His smokery for bacon, hams, etc. is a room about twelve feet square, built of *dry* wood; a fire-place in the middle, the roof conical, with nails in the rafters to hang meat intended to be smoaked. In this case a fire is made on the floor in the middle of the building in the morning, which it is not necessary to renew during the day. This is done for four or five days successively. The vent for the smoke is through the crevices of the boards. The meat is never taken out till it is used. If the walls are of stone, or green wood, the meat is apt to mould."

The unique, savory taste of Virginia hams appealed to everyone from colonials—according to common lore, there was "scarcely a Virginia lady" who did not start her day with some cured ham for breakfast—all the way into the next century and to Queen Victoria herself.

The process of getting a colonial pig from its day-to-day existence all the way to the breakfast table of a "Virginia lady" or the queen was easier said than done, especially in the early years of the seventeenth century before Williamsburg was established and traditional domestication of livestock became common practice. In those shaping years, the main reason farmers put up fences was to keep livestock out, not in. Labor was needed for the tobacco fields, not the tending of livestock, so the animals were simply left to fend for themselves in the woods and marsh. Generally, the livestock did fine, but the practice created some problems for the farmers.

Obviously, the situation made keeping up with one's livestock a near impossibility. Detailing an account of his property in 1662, prior to a voyage to England, Robert Cole acknowledged that the "number of my hoggs is uncertain butt of them that come home I thinke there is twenty nine of them and four

young piggs." Virginia planter Robert Beverley was evidently perturbed by such a careless approach to property. In Virginia, he reported, "when an Inventory of any considerable Man's Estate is taken by the Executors, the Hogs are left out, and not listed in the Appraisement." At least the farmers could search freely: in the 1640s, the Virginia General Assembly passed a law allowing livestock owners to "seake or fetch his owne cattle and hoggs from off any mans land."

Another problem was the unrestricted breeding of animals in the wild. "Hogs swarm like Vermine upon the Earth," observed Beverley, "find[ing] their own Support in the Woods, without any Care of the Owner." With so many unrestricted animals on the loose, the obvious temptation was in play. Hog stealing was "a generall crime usually comitted and seldom or never detected or prosecuted." Gangs of feral sows and piglets, cows and calves could be dangerous to colonists when mothers perceived a threat to their young. But, there were so many indigenous animals roaming around in the 1600s that feral pigs and cows were just a few more four-footed creatures in the wild. In his account of his 1669–1670 exploratory travels through Virginia and the Carolinas, John Lederer wrote,

"These Thickets harbour all sorts of beasts of prey, as Wolves, Panthers, Leopards, Lions, &c. . . . and small Vermine, as wilde Cats, Foxes, Racoons."

John Smith wrote fascinating reports of the plant and animal life he found in the New World in the early 1600s, and the "time of discovery" extended into the 1700s as Europeans gradually reached the Appalachian plateau in far southwestern Virginia. It was not exactly an enchanted fairy-tale forest. In his journal of a 1669 trip, John Lederer described seeing a mountain lion killing a deer: "Travelling thorow the Woods, a Doe seized by a wild Cat crossed our way; the miserable creature being even spent and breathless with the burden and cruelty of her rider, who having fastned on her shoulder, left not sucking out her bloud until she sunk under him: . . . This creature is something bigger than our English Fox, of a reddish grey colour, and in figure every way agreeing with an ordinary

Cat; fierce, ravenous and cunning for finding the Deer (upon which they most delight to prey) too swift for them, they watch upon branches of trees, and as they walk or feed under, jump down upon them."

Good grief. Somebody round up the livestock and get it to a safe pen. Pronto.

Free-range husbandry continued in the region throughout the 1700s, but, by the time Williamsburg was founded in 1699, practices were changing. Progressive farmers in the lower Tidewater began penning cattle to accumulate

manure. Others kept them in stalls to fatten them for market. Big planters began using draft animals more often as they converted tobacco fields to wheat and maize due to international grain demand. The greater use of draft animals to plow these fields in turn created a need for more and more livestock feed. It just became logical for a farmer to keep his livestock close at hand. Over time, it became common to fence in domestic livestock, and Virginia farms began to look and operate more like their English templates.

Civilized or not, there were certainly plenty of farmers. By the end of the eighteenth century, only about 7 percent of the nation's population lived in communities of 2,500 people or more. The rest—93 percent—dwelt closer to the land. Unless told otherwise, guests visiting Colonial Williamsburg's Historic Area might not realize that most colonial-era Virginians were farmers who lived in the countryside.

Hogs were important to colonial Virginia, but something about their appearance and lifestyle relegated them to a backstage role in the colonial repertoire company. Perhaps wallowing was not as inherently impressive as an ox's imposing display of strength as it plowed a field. Admittedly, a couple of snorting pigs lack the glamour of a matched set of black Canadian horses pulling a crested coach. Bacon comes in somewhat lower on the flash scale than a Leicester sheep supplying wool for the governor's cloak, but, still, it is so often the bit players that make a production work.

AT LEAST HOGS WERE NOT ALONE IN THE LOW LIGHT. Chickens had a ticket, but not in the VIP section. A little unfair because chickens and other

poultry contributed in many ways: cleaning up behind the more important meat and draft animals; supplying meat, eggs, feathers, and down; fertilizing the garden with their manure; and keeping all manner of pesky insects at bay.

As evidence of poultry's lowly status during the eighteenth century, its existence was usually not even mentioned in farm stock listings. Contrary to that notion, however, at Nomini Hall in Westmoreland County, Frances Carter, wife of Robert Carter, listed chickens, ducks, geese, and turkeys among the "domestic Poultry" under her care. After the death of Governor Botetourt, "20 turkeys, 18 geese, 9 ducks" were listed as part of his estate. Glaring by its omission, though, is the number of chickens in the governor's inventory. No less than Thomas Jefferson, however, seemed interested in the welfare of his chickens, as evidenced by a letter written by Jefferson to his

Red Dorking

granddaughter Ellen Wayles Randolph in 1807: "How go on the bantams?" he asked. "I rely on you for their care, as I do on Anne for the Algerine fowls, and on our arrangements at Monticello for the East Indians. These varieties are pleasant for the table and furnish an agreeable diversification in our domestic occupations."

Poultry lucky enough to be owned by well-to-do planters most likely was housed in protective shelters. Chickens belonging to smaller farmers and city dwellers were more on their own. As a rule, they were not provided any housing and were driven to roost in the orchards and woods. It is possible that some city fowl may have been sheltered in outbuildings or even in homes, but such arrangements were outside the norm.

It was not unusual for masters to allow rural slaves to tend small gardens, and some were given permission to raise their own poultry. After perusing slave quarters in Virginia, Englishman Isaac Weld wrote: "Adjoining their little habitations, the slaves commonly have small gardens and yards for poultry, which are all their own property. . . . Their gardens are generally found well stocked, and their flocks of poultry numerous."

Some slaves were able to raise excess product on which they could conceivably turn a profit. If in reasonable proximity to a city, their products could be sold in the town market. Some slaves sold directly to their masters; others found customers in their nearby neighbors. Chesapeake planter James Mercer wrote that

the slaves "are the general Chicken merchants" in his area. As such, the slaves sold chickens and eggs as food for the tables of others. In addition, poultry was an important dietary supplement for the slaves themselves.

Most masters limited their slaves to the raising of chickens only, no other poultry. This restriction was in effect at George Washington's Mount Vernon and was noticed by a visitor in 1797: "A small vegetable garden was situated close to the hut. Five or six hens, each with ten or fifteen chickens, walked around there. That is the only pleasure allowed to Negroes: they are not permitted to keep either ducks or geese or pigs."

Chickens were quite common in the confines of the colonial capital city. Although little documentation confirms specific chicken breeds, representative samples of several very old races of chickens strut about the Historic Area today: Dominique, Hamburg, Dorking,

and Nankin bantam. Of this list, only the Dominique is listed as critically endangered by the American Livestock Breeds Conservancy.

Dominiques were well-known in the colonies. A medium-sized yet robust bird, the Dominique fares quite well in the Virginia environs. Even the sometimes relatively harsh winters have little effect on the bird, whose plumage insulates it from freezing temperatures. The Dominique matures quickly and is a prolific egg layer. Along with the eggs, the Dominique's feathers, meat, and longevity probably made it a popular fowl in colonial times.

The Hamburg is an ancient breed of Dutch origin, but the Hamburgs seen in the Historic Area today are cosmetically different from their colonial-era ancestors. The variances can be traced to English farmers and others interested in fowl-breeding experimentation who strove to fine-tune "pheasant fowl" around a hundred years ago. The Hamburg was thought of as an ornamental fowl although it is an active forager and holds its own in egg production. Only the

Dominiques

Silver-Spangled Hamburg is in evidence in the Historic Area, but the breed comes in a variety of other colors.

When one contemplates ancient history, chickens do not often enter the equation, but the Dorking chicken has been around and domesticated for a very long time. The breed has a distinctive and unusual five-toed foot that was mentioned by Pliny in AD 77. Those five-toed feet are at the end of very short legs that support a rectangular body. A docile breed, the Dorking wins points as a good egg layer and an excellent mother to its chicks. Colonial Williamsburg keeps Red Dorkings, but the birds can be found elsewhere in shades of white, silver, and other colors.

Nankin bantams

Nankin bantam chickens, sometimes called *Nankeens,* were also in evidence during the time of Pliny. These miniature chickens were called *yellow bantams* in colonial times. The name *yellow* was changed to *buff* and then *Nankin,* after buff-colored cloth became an import from Nanking, China, in the midnineteenth century. Sir John Sebright is believed to have used Nankins in the development of his famous Sebright bantams. Handsome birds, the rose comb sets off a buff or gold body color and shiny black main tail feathers. Of the chicken breeds showcased by Colonial Williamsburg, the Nankin bantams are the most recently introduced.

PIGEONS, OR DOVES, WERE ANOTHER domestic food source popular both in the city and in outlying areas. The birds were housed in compartmented nesting houses or boxes called *dovecotes*. Squabs, fledgling pigeons about four weeks old, could be harvested practically year-round from these freestanding structures and/or adjuncts to existing buildings. The young birds were scooped directly from the nests when needed for a meal. According to Hill Carter, the current proprietor of Shirley Plantation, "Most were captured just a few days before they could fly away. Older birds were tough and not attractive for the dinner table. Most birds were roasted, as were quail, duck, or most any kind of wild bird."

Locating a dovecote adjacent to a house was not without problems. Despite a generous daily serving of grain, pigeons were drawn to the vegetable garden. No sooner did they break through the ground than

Giant American Crested

shoots of spinach, turnips, kale, and other vegetables were routinely snapped up by pigeons. On June 16, 1760, Col. James Gordon of Lancaster County, Virginia, wrote, "Planting peas the second time, the pigeons had pulled them up."

It was routine to see dovecotes in colonial Virginia, and, like a modern-day swimming pool or finished basement, they appear to have added value to real estate. William Fitzhugh's estate in Westmoreland County in the 1680s had "four good Cellars, a Dairy, Dovecote, Stable, Barn, Hen house[,] Kitchen & all other conveniencys." A century later, an advertisement placed in the September 24, 1767, *Virginia Gazette* listed a tract of land "within three miles of Williamsburg" for sale. Along with "two good new quarters, a very fine barn, stable, cow house, corn house, and good well," a "pigeon house" was also touted.

The wooden dovecote that still stands on the grounds of the elegant George Wythe House in the Historic Area might strike some as incongruous or even slightly out of place, but there was a societal and practical reason for it. Despite living in one of the fanciest houses in Williamsburg, Wythe, like most Virginians of the time, made a concentrated effort to be independent when it came to supplying meat and produce for his home.

The Wythe cote sits on stilts over a dozen feet tall. The height helps discourage unwelcome and deadly predators in the form of weasels and foxes. Forty-eight nesting pairs of pigeons can be accommodated in the three rows of pigeonholes that run around the inside of the house. To provide easy access for a

pigeon master or cook, back doors are located in the one-foot-deep nests or cubbyholes.

Adding validity to our image of doves as snow-white symbols of peace, these birds evidently thrived in a clean, whitewashed environment. As was reported in the 1755 *Country Gentleman's Companion,* "They must have their Rooms and Boxes made clean once a Week, for they delight much in Neatness; and if the Walls be outwardly whited or painted, they love it the better, for they delight much in fair Buildings."

For rich planters and successful city dwellers, a dovecote could be an architectural sensation and structure of great beauty. The grandiose brick dovecote at Shirley Plantation, dating from 1723–1738, is both a work of art and utilitarian. The vast majority of common-folk dovecotes, however, were of unpainted wood, post-in-ground construction. That efficient but not made-for-the-ages building technique resulted in most of the dovecotes falling down after a generation or two—a logical explanation as to why so few of them are standing today.

William Byrd's Falling Creek plantation dovecote became so essential to Byrd's lifestyle that it was raised up on pillars to prevent rot. One wonders why Byrd (1674–1744) needed a dovecote at all as it was reported in 1737 that "one finds here such a terrible number of wild doves that their great, enormous flocks, whenever they fly from the country, darken the sun for quite a while, and when they want to rest in the woods, they break the branches because of their numbers."

Humans have had a relationship with pigeons for thousands of years. The birds are versatile in terms of shape, size, color, and feather ornamentation and have long been prized for their meat, competitions, entertainment, and production of a valuable manure. Three pigeon breeds are on-site in Colonial Williamsburg's Historic Area: Runt, Giant Homer, and Giant American Crested.

Probably one of the first breeds imported into colonial America, the Runt is also one of the oldest recorded pigeons. Latin writers described the breed more than two thousand years ago. It is known as the Roman pigeon in Europe. The Runt has been used to increase the size of most utilitarian breeds as it, despite its name, is one of the largest of the pigeon breeds.

Runt

Williamsburg's eighteenth-century residents never confused poultry raised for the table with fowl raised specifically for cockfighting. The care of kitchen-bound poultry fell under domestic duties and thus was women's work. The raising and training of gamecocks was a job performed overwhelmingly by men.

Cockfighting was a sport enjoyed by gentry and slaves and all classes in between. It was less expensive, after all, to keep gamecocks than racehorses. The birds provided an opportunity for those with lighter purses to participate in animal gaming. As with horse racing, preparations for the cocking seasons continued year-round, and significant amounts of money passed hands once bets were on.

Capitalizing on the inherent territoriality of roosters in general, and gamecocks in particular, cockers develop elaborate training strategies for their roosters. Regular exercise and a specialized diet help prepare feathered warriors for the pit. On reaching maturity, the birds are set out in individual pens, or walks, with a few females. For the same reason that a dog will lift his leg to mark his territory, a rooster will crow. It establishes his dominance within the range of his voice. The rooster crows to announce a challenge to would-be rivals: "My hens and my territory. Keep out!"

Cockers maximize a rooster's aggression in sparring matches with other gamecocks. Without interference, mature roosters will fight one another, but most often the fight lasts only as long as it takes for one of them to back down. In training gamecocks, cockers incite the birds to fight beyond normal limits, conditioning them to continue striking the opponent. The battle in the cockpit is usually a fight to the death. Colonial aficionados described cockfights as valiant and heroic. To say of a gamecock "he took his death with valor" was the highest praise afforded a loser in the pit.

These sporting fowl are a breed apart, raised and trained specifically for the pit or, in the case of game hens, as breeders of fighting birds. With its specialized diet and regular exercise, the gamecock would be a lean, tough, and sinewy offering on the dinner table.

Different generations have applied varying value to the utilitarian aspects of the chicken. Cockfighting has gone up and down in popularity over the years; most twenty-first-century Americans regard it with decided distaste. Feather beds have had their own turn going from a must-have to old hat. Chicken as a meal has bloomed in certain decades, waned in others.

One thing has remained constant throughout the centuries, however. People like eggs: scrambled, fried, boiled, in an omelet, as an ingredient in most anything. Eggs were a popular food in the colonial era, and into the twenty-first

century there has been no letup in demand. Eggs are at once one of nature's divine creations and most baffling mysteries. How does it work?

The laying cycle of a hen, like that of most birds, is dictated by the amount of light to which it is exposed. During the shorter days of winter, fresh eggs are scarce. As spring settles in with increasing daylight hours, a hen's reproductive system goes into full production. Contrary to popular belief, a rooster isn't needed for a hen to lay eggs. He is necessary only if those eggs are to be fertilized to produce more chickens.

A similar misconception is that fertile eggs taken from a nest will contain a developing chick. If the eggs are being gathered daily, this simply is not possible. Fertile eggs will not develop unless they are incubated. A brooding hen's warm body provides this incubation.

Broodiness is the term describing a hen's inclination to sit on a clutch, or nest, of eggs around the clock until the eggs hatch. It is unclear exactly what triggers a hen to become broody, but, oddly enough, mathematics appears to play a role. Most hens will not sit a nest until it contains a particular number of eggs. Take, for example, a hen that goes broody when she has a dozen eggs in her nest. She lays her first egg on the first day of the month. She then lays one egg a day until the twelfth day of the month, at which time broodiness sets in. Even if several hens lay their eggs in the same nest, accumulating the mysterious number of eggs to trigger broodiness can take time because each hen lays only one egg a day.

A broody hen will usually stop laying and, within a few days, settle onto her clutch and remain there for the next twenty-one days. She will leave only for brief periods to eat and drink. She may pluck the feathers from her breast creating a bare space of skin called a *brood patch*. By removing these feathers from the area of her body that comes in contact with the eggs, she ensures that her body heat will be delivered directly to her eggs.

Several times a day she will roll, or turn, the eggs beneath her with her beak. She will pull in ones that may be outside the protective warmth of her body, fluffing her feathers to give her clutch full coverage as she settles down. This egg rolling is critical. If an egg remains stationary, all its internal weight bears down on a single part of the developing chick's body, restricting blood flow to that area and possibly stunting the growth of a wing, leg, or internal organ.

If all the eggs are fertile, they will hatch within a twenty-four-hour period on the twenty-first day of incubation. The egg laid on the first of the month will be just as viable as the egg laid on the twelfth day even though the former was in the nest nearly two weeks before the hen sat it. In fact, it could have lain three weeks before being incubated and still produce a healthy chick.

Unlike many birds, chickens do not leave the nest to seek food to feed their hatchlings. Instead, the hen takes her young out to scratch and forage for their

food just as she does. Nourished by the nutrient-rich yolk of the eggs they formerly inhabited, the chicks can afford several days of limited success in feeding themselves as they gain strength and learn just how it is done.

To ensure a steady supply of eggs year-round, giant modern-day chicken farms alter natural schedules, trick hens with artificial light, and replace foraging with processed, enhanced feed. Left to their own devices, however, a chicken is a chicken and it does and did just fine, thank you, in the Williamsburg chicken runs of today and yesterday.

When it came to poultry as a dinner item, the trip from barnyard to barbeque was a relatively easy procedure: grab bird, kill bird, clean bird, cook bird, eat bird. Yet, there was a lot of sirloin, mutton, and pork chop on the hoof all over the fields and forests of colonial Virginia. How did the prime rib actually get to the fine china on Mr. Wythe's polished table? What process put the bacon on a blacksmith's tin plate?

Early on, when nearly everyone in colonial Virginia lived on farms, the meat supply was a contained operation. Subsistence farmers raised a variety of livestock for multiple purposes, and the animals were slaughtered when they proved no longer useful for providing milk, wool, reproduction, or traction. What these hardscrabble farmers slaughtered, they consumed.

By the early eighteenth century, fifty to seventy-five households in town created enough demand for meat that larger planters began raising excess animals for sale at market. It was a welcome source of new income

for larger planters living within one to two hours travel time of Williamsburg. By the late 1730s, these big planters had emerged as the primary suppliers of meat.

Meat was a very large part of the colonial Virginian's diet. Soldiers and free male laborers, for example, were allotted a pound of meat a day. By 1769, local plantations and farmers could not supply the annual 300,000 to 450,000 pounds of meat Williamsburg required. To satisfy their meat needs, Williamsburg residents turned to more distant sources. The surplus production of some hundreds of farmers living within a hundred-mile radius helped meet requirements. Soon, it was not unusual for meat raised across the James River to be brought to Williamsburg. In at least one case, the product was driven in over two hundred miles from the West.

Early on, the actual mechanics of the meat industry were in a free-for-all state. Without municipal government dictates, the slaughtering, butchering, and selling of meat could be done essentially anywhere. But, as the chaos grew, with more and more city dwellers buying rather than raising their meat and the ranks

of meat sellers steadily increasing, city governments began designating locations where livestock could be slaughtered. Additional regulation defined which parts of the slaughtered animals could be legally sold to the public. Butchering became big business.

As the urban market for meat developed, shopkeepers saw an opportunity and soon became as important a source for the products as were the big planters. In many instances, storekeepers simply accepted and resold poultry, game, and bigger livestock offered by customers as barter for imported goods. They would also seek out and purchase cattle and pigs to add to the products in their stores.

By the last quarter of the eighteenth century, the days of town households subsisting completely on meats they produced themselves were over. Wealthy people still supplied meat from their own plantations, but professionals—doctors, lawyers, ministers, teachers, and government officials—purchased much of their meat from big planters and middlemen. Probably by prior arrangement, planters supplied

customers with pork, beef, veal, mutton, and lamb. Smaller animals were sold mostly in the form of freshly killed whole animals; bigger beasts by the quarter or the side. Even though consumers today would consider a side or quarter of an animal to be a huge quantity of meat, householders and businesspeople could best use and afford to pay for these quantities brought in from the big plantations. Other professionals, depending on their connections and their needs, bought from the big planters or they bought smaller cuts of meat from shopkeepers and other middlemen.

A few tradespeople had nearby farms, but most depended on commercial sources. Public markets, butchers, and shopkeepers were practically the only sources from which tradespeople and less well-off townsfolk could purchase their meat. To this segment of the population, prices were nearly out of reach, reflecting a generous markup by the middlemen. Vendors set prices without restriction, "which [are] generally exorbitant enough," remarked one critic, "especially on publick times, or when little meat is at market." To add insult to injury, evidence suggests that the quality of the meats sold in public markets was sometimes, to be kind, subpar. The same critic observed "meat for poverty not fit to eat, and sometimes almost spoiled" hanging too long in the Williamsburg public market.

Still, one or more liberal servings of nonpoultry meat every day was something some individuals and families simply did not intend to go without. Most colonial diners had a protein-rich diet thanks to the ready availability of meat of one description or another. In addition, fish played a nutritional and recreational role.

FISHING WAS POPULAR FOR BOTH FOOD AND SPORT. In early colonial Virginia, before livestock really took hold, fish quickly became a diet staple. As the eighteenth century wore on, fish were still an important food source, but, at least where the elite were concerned, the amount eaten was nowhere near that of beef, pork, or mutton. Still, the more subjective appeal of lazing by a clear stream with a pole and a line in the water struck a timeless chord. One can easily speculate that, had bumper stickers been around in the 1700s, more than one cart, coach, or equine flank would have sported an "I'd rather be fishing" banner.

The diversity of fishing methods and profusion of fish were described by Robert Beverley around 1705: "The Indian Invention of Weirs [a fence or enclosure set in a waterway for catching fish] in Fishing, is mightily improved by the English besides which, they make use of Seins, Trolls, Casting-Netts, Setting-Netts, Hand-fishing, and Angling, and in each find abundance of Diversion. I have set in the shade, at the Heads of Rivers Angling, and spent as much time in taking the Fish off the Hook, as in waiting for their taking it. Like those of the Euxine Sea, they also Fish with Spilyards, which is a long Line staked out in the River, and hung with a great many Hooks on short strings, fasten'd to the main Line, about three or four Foot asunder. The only difference is, our Line is supported by Stakes, and theirs is buoyed up with Gourds."

Colonials enjoyed a variety of fish, including black drum, sheepshead, red drum, rockfish, white perch, catfish, and gar. The most popular, though, appears to have been sturgeon. The sturgeon is an anadromous fish, which means it spends most of its life in brackish or salt water but migrates into coastal rivers to spawn. The Jamestown colonists reported that sturgeon were plentiful in the James River from May until September. John Smith was probably referring to sturgeon when, in 1624, he observed "fish, lying so thicke with their heads above the water, as for want of nets (our barge driving amongst them) we attempted to catch them with a frying pan: but we found it a bad instrument to catch fish with." According to the 1610 *True Declaration of the Estate of the Colonie in Virginia*, Thomas Gates reported to the Council of Virginia, "The riuer swarmeth with Sturgeon." Archaeology also supports the prevalence of sturgeon.

Though totally lacking in any kind of *Field and Stream*–like quality, some innovative techniques for catching sturgeon were dreamed up by colonials and natives alike. For example, Native Americans in Beverley's time clapped a noose over the tail of the big fish, gripped the other end of the rope, and—swimming, wading, and diving—held on for dear life until the fish was finally on shore.

Sturgeon demanded innovative fishing techniques. The giants could weigh up to 800 pounds, reach lengths of up to 15 feet, and live 60 years.

The Marquis de Chastellux happened upon some Virginians using yet another outside-the-box if not vaguely unsportsmanlike sturgeon fishing system. "As I was walking by the riverside, I saw two negroes carrying an immense sturgeon, and on my asking them how they had taken it, they told me that at this season, they were so common as to be taken easily in a sean (a sort of fishing-net), and that fifteen or twenty were found sometimes in the net; but that there was a much more simple method of taking them, which they had just been using. This species of monsters, which are so active in the evening as to be perpetually leaping to a great height above the surface of the water, usually sleep profoundly at mid-day. Two or three negroes then proceed in a little boat, furnished with a long cord, at the end of which is a sharp iron crook, which they hold suspended like a log line. As soon as they find this line stopped by some obstacle, they draw it forcibly towards them, so as to strike the hook into the sturgeon, which they either drag out of the water, or which, after some struggling, and losing all its blood, floats at length upon the surface, and is easily taken."

Sturgeon was plentiful in Chesapeake rivers until the mid-nineteenth century when it began to disappear. The value of its roe, American caviar, brought on its near destruction in the late 1800s. The news was even worse fifty years later: by the 1940s, after decades of near extinction, most Virginians had little or no knowledge of the once prolific sturgeon. In the decades since, sturgeon has made somewhat of a comeback in more northern climes, and conservation efforts are under way to restore significant numbers of the historic fish to Chesapeake waters.

The amount of fishing that was done in colonial Virginia is exemplified by orders for equipment. Merchants in colonial Virginia provided for quantity as well as diversification. Hooks dedicated to a full range of fish from perch to trout were purchased by the gross. Storekeepers ordered trout lines by the dozens. Individuals also stocked up on fishing equipment. Botanist John Clayton's fishing needs confirm the popularity of the exercise. Included in his annual orders from England were dozens of trout, perch, and sheepshead hooks and trout lines.

Colonial cooks were every bit as creative as the rope-throwing, hook-setting, frying pan–wielding fishermen. The taverns boomed, and meal gatherings, plain and fancy, were commonplace. Naturally, one had to first get to the tavern or party venue. More often than not, that trip involved arguably the most significant animal of the colonial period, the horse.

EVERY BREED—FROM A PAMPERED THOROUGHBRED dining on good oats in its squire's stable to a hard-working draft animal tugging a plow through hard ground in the rain—made a contribution. It would not be too big a stretch to say the colonies were built on the high spirits, hard hooves, and smooth muscles of horses.

With Devon cattle and Leicester sheep safely in the fields and folds of Colonial Williamsburg, the Rare Breeds program turned its attention to horses. Although Virginia is noted for its fine racing horses, a more diverse stock dominated the city, as evidenced in the range of descriptions in the May 19, 1774, issue of Clementina Rind's *Virginia Gazette:* "STRAYED, or stolen, from the subscriber, in Williamsburg, on Sunday the 1st of May, a white mare, about 13 hands one or two inches high. . . . TAKEN up, in Culpeper, a black horse, about 4 feet 8 or 9 inches high . . . has a small star in his forehead, and branded on the near shoulder and buttock. . . . TAKEN up, in Dunmore, a dark bay mare."

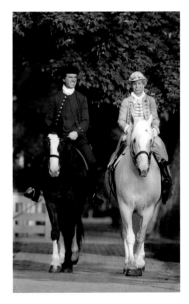

Horses of every color, size, and description were everywhere.

Whether privately owned or for hire, horses moved travelers to and from the capital city every day of the week. People came to town for serious business and casual pleasure; for visiting and family matters; for market days, court days, and church. A wide variety of horses pulled a diverse collection of wagons and coaches, but many of these animals were simply saddled up and ridden.

Traveling on horseback was the preferred method of transport for a number of Virginia's burgesses when attending sessions at the Capitol in Williamsburg. With a portmanteau attached to the back of the saddle to carry fresh shirts,

stockings, and other items, this method of travel was efficient and economical. George Washington noted in his diary that he could travel from his Mount Vernon home to Williamsburg (about 150 miles) in three days if he made only a few stops along the way.

Traveling through Virginia in 1770, J. F. D. Smyth, recently arrived from Scotland, commented, "Indeed nothing can be more elegant and beautiful than the horses bred here, either for the turf, the field, the road, or the coach."

It would be impossible to identify every breed of horse that ever trudged, trotted, or cantered along the streets of colonial Williamsburg. Nonetheless, the Rare Breeds program wanted to inject the spirit of the program into the modern-day stables. To that end, the Coach and Livestock staff investigated horse breeds that were representative of the era and also in real danger of falling by the modern wayside.

As a result of that research, two rare breeds, the American Cream Draft horse and the Canadian, now work alongside their unthreatened brethren in the Historic Area. Both breeds are listed as critically endangered by the American Livestock Breeds Conservancy.

American Cream Drafts

The American Cream Draft horse is a beautiful animal of rich cream color, amber eyes, and white tail and mane. It is the only draft-horse breed originating in America. Although it is a twentieth-century breed, it is similar in stature and appearance to certain varieties of the eighteenth century. Because of its friendly disposition, impressive appearance, alertness, and strength, the American Cream Draft is ideal for wagons, carts, and field work throughout the Historic Area.

Bred for field work and heavy labor, American Creams all but disappeared with the mechanization of agriculture. The story of this horse vividly illustrates how altered expectations can be the death knell for domestic animals. As the tractor gained popularity on the farm, the need for horses to plow and haul began to fade away. American Creams, along with many other draft breeds, fell from favor and slowly began to disappear. When the mares Mary and Jane,

Jane's colt Moses, and stallion Silver were introduced into the Rare Breeds program in 1989, there were only about twenty-five of these animals registered in the United States.

The story of the American Cream also showcases how the Rare Breeds program can positively affect long-term survival. Between 1989 and 2004, an additional 396 were registered. The two Creams currently owned by the Foundation were born here. The promotional aspects of this still critically rare breed's presence in Colonial Williamsburg's Historic Area can only positively influence the future of the magnificent American Cream.

Etienne Faillon wrote an apt description of the Canadian horse in 1865: "Small, but robust, hocks of steel, thick mane floating in the wind, bright and lively eyes, pricking its sensitive ears at the least noise, going along day and night with the same courage, wide awake beneath its harness; spirited, good, gentle, affectionate, following his road with the finest instinct to come surely home to his own stable. Such were the horses of our fathers."

Canadians

In its early years, the Canadian earned a reputation as "the little iron horse" due to its strength and toughness. A calm, docile disposition compliments its physical prowess and adaptability. A horse of medium build, the Canadian is usually black (sometimes brown, bay, or chestnut) with a full, long, wavy mane and tail, evidence of its Barb and Andalusian ancestry.

Documentation indicates that the breed was imported into the colonies during the seventeenth and eighteenth centuries. The combination of the Canadian's physical and historical attributes made the decision to bring the breed to Williamsburg an easy one. The first Canadian horses, Juliette and Gizzelle, were brought into the Rare Breeds program in 1997.

For the Rare Breeds program, there is also the satisfaction of helping to restore a breed whose numbers had dwindled to less than four hundred by 1976. Its demise is surprising when stacked up against the Canadian's near-critical importance for so

Chariots (above), post chariot (opposite)

long. The breed could be counted on for riding, drawing an elegant carriage or drab dray, even pulling a plow. Stagecoach routes, Civil War cavalry, West Indies sugar plantations, and everything in between relied on this utility breed.

Despite being the "go to" horse for so long, exportation, huge Civil War casualties, and machines on the farm nearly eradicated the Canadian horse. Numbers have increased since the four hundred in 1976, but the breed is still listed as critically endangered. Thanks in part to Colonial Williamsburg's Rare Breeds program, however, the future looks brighter for the noble Canadian.

Whether galloping along on a graceful Canadian's back or making plodding progress in a cart pulled by a draft horse, travel in the colonies was often a challenge. As in modern day, a good part of a successful journey depended on the equipment used.

The chaise or chariot was the most common four-wheeled carriage owned in colonial Virginia, with the coach a close second. On the chaise, the coachman's seat could be easily removed, thus rendering it a *post chaise* (or *post chariot*). The name comes from the position of the driver as a postilion rider, mounted on the

Coach

Riding chair

left, or nearside, horse. Though a coach could accommodate four to six passengers, the post chaise, with its single seat for up to three travelers and no coachman's seat, was favored for longer distances because its lighter weight allowed for easier pulling over rough roads. The post chaise was also much safer and more comfortable for the driver, as colonial Virginia's roads were notoriously harsh on wheeled vehicles and the coachman's seat did not have springs or suspension. This rough ride could cause significant discomfort over a long haul. In addition, each rut and hole in the road had the potential to throw the coachman from his seat, especially at higher speeds.

Distance travel was not everyone's concern. Indeed, residents of Williamsburg on their daily business about the town walked more often than they rode, and many of the vehicles seen in Williamsburg were riding chairs, carts, and the like as opposed to post chaises and coaches.

The horses of Virginia played a very important role from the outset of the Revolution. As early as June 1776, a volunteer cavalry battalion was formed for

the defense of the commonwealth. Known briefly as Bland's Virginia Horse, in reference to the unit's commander, Theodorick Bland, the unit was officially mustered into the Continental Army in March 1777 and became the First Continental Light Dragoons. In addition to their combat duties in the cavalry, horses, of course, provided general transportation for everyone from generals to lowly messengers. Horses also played a significant role in the colonies' struggle by transporting equipment and supplies to the front lines during the six-year engagement of the American Revolution.

Cart

Since horses were such a big daily presence and filled many crucial roles in colonial Virginia, the sheer numbers of the animals required some order. Although ear notches became a common way of establishing ownership of some livestock, horses were branded. It was expected, of course, that livestock in town, including horses, be stabled or kept secure within fences. As we've seen, such was not always the case in the country.

Allowing livestock to roam free in the countryside had numerous disadvantages, one of which was the necessity of locating these same animals from time to time. In *The Present State of Virginia* (1724), Hugh Jones, a professor at the College of William and Mary, noted the rather humorous task of locating horses: "They [Virginians] are such lovers of riding, that almost every ordinary person keeps a horse; and I have known some spend the morning in ranging several miles in the woods to find and catch their horses only to ride two or three miles to church, to the court-house, or to a horse-race."

Horse racing was one of Virginia's favorite diversions. In fact, Williamsburg's racetrack was conveniently located just a short distance east of the Capitol, now the site of Quarterpath Park, a community recreation area. This oval track was similar to a typical English racetrack: up to two miles long, laid out in a circular pattern. Such a track could host distance races of any length, simply determined by how many circuits the horses were required to run. Most heats were three to five miles in distance. Obviously, this type of racing called for endurance rather than flat-out speed.

A departure from distance racing was the quarter-mile, or quarter-path, race. This popular diversion was first established in Virginia and North Carolina in the seventeenth century. While true that distance racing was enjoyed in the colony, spectators found the excitement of the quarter-path horse race hard to match.

Thomas Anburey, a British officer in Virginia during the Revolutionary War, was witness to a typical quarter-mile race near Charlottesville: "Quarter-racing . . . is a match between two horses, to run a quarter of a mile in a straight direction . . . this diversion is a great favorite of the middling and lower classes, and they have a breed of horses to perform it with astonishing velocity." He noted that English-bred racing horses would be no match for the Virginia stock "for our horses are some time before they are able to get into full speed, and these are trained to set out in that manner the moment of starting."

These same fleet-footed horses, called *quarter-path racing horses,* which were bred for the quarter-mile track, are the foundation stock of the American Quarter Horse, the first breed of horse native to the United States.

Virginians took horse racing, quarter mile or distance course, very seriously. Some wagered small fortunes on the outcome of a single match. Although Anburey pointed out that racing was "a great favorite" of the middling and lower

classes, it was the gentry that could devote the necessary resources to breeding, training, and even importing top-notch racing stock.

Most of Virginia's racing stock has Thoroughbred roots. In the case of quarter-path racehorses, many eighteenth-century champions could trace their pedigrees to the stud Janus, imported in 1756.

Venture and risk were as much a part of horse racing's appeal as was the pleasure of the sport. The opportunity to make or lose substantial amounts of money was found on and off the track. Like the great Kentucky horse farms of today, making a champion racehorse available for breeding purposes after its racing prime could be a very profitable endeavor for the steed's owner.

Horses were such an integral part of the colonial-era mosaic that no representation of those times would be complete without homage to them. It is in that spirit that the Colonial Williamsburg Foundation treasures its horses for both their unassailable link to the past and their very real day-to-day contribution to the Historic Area experience.

Every workplace has to contend with the unexpected. Workers may become ill and need to stay at home; they may suffer injury and have their work duties temporarily reduced. When these workers are horses, the humans who care for them not only pick up the slack and cover the change in plan but also take full responsibility for the care and recovery of their equine charges.

Morning at Colonial Williamsburg's Coach and Livestock facility begins as early as six thirty when the stable grooms arrive to fetch and feed the horses scheduled for work that day. Typically, the horses have either spent the night in one of the numerous pastures found in and around the Historic Area or slept in stalls at the stable.

A chart in the feed room informs the grooms about the particular diet of each horse. The rations are carefully monitored for maximum benefit based on the animal's age, weight, and individual health history. As the horses finish their breakfast, the coachmen arrive to ready the teams. The horses are thoroughly washed, groomed, and harnessed. The coachmen then don their eighteenth-century livery, hitch their teams to carriages, and proceed into the Historic Area.

Colonial Williamsburg guests can purchase tickets to experience for themselves horse-drawn transportation through the Historic Area. For those people walking the streets and grounds, the various horses at work and leisure provide an important reminder of the past. Their ancestors helped build the colonies and America.

THE CONTRIBUTIONS OF HORSES MESHED with the roles of cows, sheep, and poultry to form an efficient livestock machine. Working for their hard-driven masters brought life-sustaining results, but were there colonial animals on a more genteel and relaxed track? How about a trusty dog or affectionate cat whose only real function was to entertain and be a treasured companion? What about colonial pets?

Modern-era petting zoos might envy the wide variety of animals kept as pets in colonial Virginia. Dogs, cats, squirrels, deer, monkeys, rabbits, mockingbirds, and songbirds were all there. Bats, toads, and hedgehogs do not generally spring to mind when contemplating pets, but, evidently, even these creatures were occasionally welcome in the odd Virginia home. William Byrd recorded visiting Alexander Spotswood's home where he discovered Mrs. Spotswood and her sister playing with tame deer that were allowed to run in and out of the house at will.

Although the circumstances and level of interaction varied widely, there are records of humans keeping animals as pets as far back as written history goes. Even so, it may seem strange and oddly out of sync in today's world of dog and cat shows, specialized retail chains, and pet resorts that pets were not universally accepted by all levels of society until around the eighteenth century.

Dogs, cats, and other animals were fun pets, of course, but they were sometimes expected to carry part of the household burden as well. Many Virginia cats went about the business of rodent removal in an anonymous and unheralded way. Others seem to have been more firmly entrenched in the household. On April 26, 1780, Robert Wormley Carter noted the death of a family cat that he reasoned to have been seventeen years old: "Old Cat Coorytang. . . . was a favourite of my Fathers [Landon Carter]—and I have taken great care of him on that account—tho' very troublesome." Children's great fondness for kittens was the same then as now. Patriarch planter William Byrd gave his friend Drury Stith's son "a little cat to carry to his sister."

Where dogs were concerned, the Reverend John Clayton noted in 1686 that "every house keeps three or four mungril dogs to destroy vermin, such as Wolves, Foxes, Rackoons, Opossums, etc." Clayton also made mention of "little currs" for vermin and "Great Dogs" for wolves, bears, panthers, and other large beasts. The lineage of these "mungril" dogs is anybody's guess, but they were probably some mix of terrier, hound, and pick-a-breed.

The Rare Breeds program has not really had to address the issue of dogs and cats since innumerable breeds available today are the same as those that roamed colonial streets or purred in a warm colonial lap. Advertisements for lost or stolen animals in the eighteenth-century *Virginia Gazette* mention bulldogs, mastiffs, pointers, and Pomeranians among others. Even Lord Dunmore's dogs were not safe. In April 1774, he reported in the *Virginia Gazette* that his bulldog "Glasgow" and two pointer puppies had been stolen and offered a twenty-shilling reward for each one's return.

Apparently, Williamsburg was teeming with uncontrolled dogs in 1772. So much so that "An Act to prevent Mischief from DOGS" was passed to help shield city dwellers from "fierce Dogs, and others, in too great Num-

bers running at large within the Limits." Dog owners were required to keep their animals chained and to fit each dog with a collar bearing the owner's initials. As a last, or perhaps first, line of defense, Williamsburg constables and citizens alike had the right to shoot dogs that were unrestrained and running wild in the city.

On the other hand, the General Assembly forbade the shooting of tame deer. The Assembly repeatedly passed acts to prevent overhunting. One passed in 1772 included deer kept as pets: Any persons who "shoot, or otherwise kill, any tame deer, having a bell or collar on its neck . . . shall be liable to an action of trespass."

Perhaps in an attempt to avoid as much gunplay as possible, some Williamsburg residents tamed more benign animals for their in-house pets. Despite their annoying habit of chewing up their benevolent owner's clothing, squirrels were mentioned in several sources as desirable and entertaining pets. One writer of the period described squirrels as "sweet sportful beasts and . . . very pleasant playfellows in a house." Even wild birds, cardinals and mockingbirds in particular, were captured and morphed into household pets.

Deer in the hallway and squirrels scampering up and down the banisters notwithstanding, dogs were still far and away the most popular pet in colonial Williamsburg. The dogs imported to Virginia during the early discovery and settlement years at Jamestown were valued for their ability to assist man. To preserve this resource, the General Assembly, in 1619, actually passed an act prohibiting dogs "of the English race" to be sold or even given as gifts to the natives. Of course, dogs being dogs, the canine population soon expanded rapidly rendering such edicts moot.

Often, the line blurred between pet dogs and those that worked for a living. In colonial Virginia, it was fine to be an affectionate companion, but, if Ole Sparky could also work, his value went up. Dogs earned their keep in many ways. One of their most marketable skills was the herding of sheep, cattle, and pigs. In the early free-range husbandry days, unfenced cattle and hogs commonly fended for themselves in marshy and wooded areas. Rounding up wild and semiwild stock was difficult, and the importance of a good stock dog was immeasurable. Chasing and turning the horned cattle required great speed, and facing a feral razorback hog mandated strength and toughness.

Dogs were also used to herd livestock to market, sometimes over quite a distance. Cattle were commonly driven thirty miles or more from outlying farms into town for market days. As the eighteenth century progressed and the western settlement boundaries expanded, herding dogs continued to be important. It was not unheard of for a master and his dogs to drive livestock from the frontier to urban markets.

The presence of dogs in all of their work, companionship, and sporting guises touched practically everyone, including the fathers of our country. George Washington, for example, received some French "shepherd dogs" from Thomas Jefferson in 1791. Washington also owned foxhounds, a powerful breed used in hunting. A friend described an incident involving one of these dogs: One of Washington's hounds, Vulcan, was an unwelcome visitor to the kitchen. A large

party of guests was being entertained at Mount Vernon. Dinner was announced, but, as the guests began taking their seats, Mrs. Washington realized the requisite ham was not on the table. The butler, Frank, cleared up the mystery. Vulcan had brazenly swiped the ham from the kitchen. Although the cooks "stood bravely to such arms as they could get . . . Vulcan had finally triumphed and bore off the prize." Like any hostess of any era, Mrs. Washington did not fully appreciate the humor in Vulcan's mischief.

Although most colonial Virginians did not technically consider foxhounds pets, the dog's breeding and training regimens were topmost of mind for many residents, George Washington among them. French General Rochambeau took to Virginia hounds as well. Sometime after the battle of Yorktown, a French officer reported that "M. De Rochambeau, who liked hunting very much, amused himself during the whole winter riding through the woods, followed by twenty or so enthusiasts. . . . the dog packs belonging to the Gentlemen of the neighborhood are wonderful. . . . the country around Williamsburg favors this kind of hunting."

Like many others, English General Lee kept dogs just for their good company. He brought along his pets when he went to visit the parents of young Helen Calvert near Norfolk. He had "four ugly little dogs, which he petted, pestered everybody with, in a nauseous style." The good general was probably not invited back to the Calvert household: "How was my good mother scandalized next morning when the maid came to her and told her that the strange General not satisfied with occupying one of the

beds himself, had actually clapped all his ugly dogs into the other."

General Lee might have been more welcome had he brought along a bird or two in a cage. As a fad, having small caged birds in the house and teaching them to sing caught on in the colonies. Virginians also kept cardinals and mockingbirds and frequently sent them to England where the colorful creatures fetched two guineas.

People of this period also thought they could teach a wild bird to sing a man-made tune. Lord Dunmore had a small barrel organ, called a *serinette,* for this purpose. Others used small English flutes called *flageolettes.* The idea was to play a song repeatedly at the same pitch, and, sooner or later, the bird would mimic the music. One can only speculate as to the success of the experiments, but something in it had England and Virginia mesmerized by the possibilities. At the very least, the birds reinforce the notion that singing creatures, indeed pets of all kinds, bring joy and somehow make things better no matter what the century.

The eighteenth century foreshadowed a more widespread practice of pet keeping and the establishment of the humane movement in the nineteenth century. There was a burgeoning belief in some quarters that kindness itself could be shaped and fostered through pets. These sentiments were best expressed by a man many forward-thinking Virginia parents considered a prophetic educator, John Locke. According to Locke, "Children should from the beginning be brought up in an abhorrence of killing or tormenting any living creature," and, "when they had them, they must be sure to keep them well and look diligently after them, that they wanted nothing or were not ill-used."

THOUGH LOCKE MADE THAT statement nearly three hundred years ago, the sentiments expressed aptly describe the credo of today's Coach and Livestock Department at the Colonial Williamsburg Foundation. The American Livestock Breeds Conservancy awarded the Colonial Williamsburg Foundation, under the leadership of Richard Nicoll, director of Coach and Livestock, its Turn of the Century Award "for his work in promoting and conserving several endangered breeds of livestock and bringing the issue before the public."

The citation further stated, "It certainly would have been easier to populate Williamsburg's fields and barns with more modern and common breeds. It would have saved time and money to use artificial insemination on the rare horses, sheep, and cattle, to avoid road trips to obtain new animals and to move breeding groups. Yet the rare breeds have paid back for the inconvenience by providing interesting topics to discuss, beautiful animals to show visitors, and the feeling that Williamsburg is helping these vulnerable populations to survive."

Randall Lineback, the latest addition to Colonial Williamsburg's Rare Breeds program

ACKNOWLEDGMENTS

THIS BOOK COULD NOT HAVE COME TO fruition without the unmatched professional talent of a number of individuals. My sincere thanks to Colonial Williamsburg's Abigail Schumann for her original concept and careful photography direction; Richard Nicoll, Elaine Shirley, Allison Harcourt, and their fellow Coach and Livestock members for their expert guidance in colonial husbandry and Colonial Williamsburg's Rare Breeds program; Linda Rowe for her untiring forays into books, manuscripts, and local museums to keep the facts on the straight and narrow; Frank Clark for his patient explanations of eighteenth-century foodways; Laura Arnold, Joanne Bowen, Jane Carson, Phyllis Dadd, Patricia Gibbs, Allison Harcourt, Mark Howell, Kevin Kelly, Kay Little, Michael Olmert, Richard Powell, and Lorena Walsh for their particular areas of expertise and publications; Joseph Rountree for his orchestration, advice, and guidance; Helen Olds for her visual artistry; Amy Watson for her unique combination of technical skill and gut instinct; Julie Watson for keeping everyone else on track; *William and Mary Quarterly* author Virginia DeJohn Anderson for information on free-range livestock; Don Bixby of the American Livestock Breeds Conservancy for information on Ossabaw Island pigs; and the numerous Colonial Williamsburg staff and others who helped in myriad and sundry ways.

In addition, this book would not be the stunning visual treat that it is without the captivating photography. The new photography staged for this book was possible thanks to the talents of the following people who served as models or provided off-camera support: Tom Austin, Erin Bendiner, Antoinette Brennan, Frances Burroughs, Dennis Cotner, Emmanuel Dabney, Debra Downs, Cristie Dressler, Mike Durling, Larry Earl, Eric Gratigni, Tom Green, Allison Harcourt, Martin Harcourt, Rachel Harcourt, Dan Hard, Tom Hay, Joyce Henry, Bridgette Houston, Jay Howlett, Carson Hudson, Eric Hunter, Mark Hutter, James Ingram, Emily James, Greg James, Preston Jones, Richard Josey, Martha Katz-Hyman, Todd Keru, Barbara Kleopfer, Bob Krasche, Robert Leath, Barbara Lombardi, Michael Lombardi, Carrie MacDougall, Ian MacDougall, Ayinda Martin, Brett McMicheal, Edward Merkley, Kelly Mihalcoe, Shari Monaco, Dan Moore, Stephen Moore, Alex Morse, Richard Nicoll, Anne Parker, Gail Peck, Lee Peters, Phyllis Putnam, Chuck Roberts, Emily Roberts, Randy Rogers, Bill Rose, Kathy Rose, Brenda Rosseau, Mark Schneider, Amanda Schumann, Claire Schumann, Elaine Shirley, DeAndre Short, DeVonte Short, Ed Shultz, Phil Schultz, Karen Smith, Stephen Southard, Olivia Spry, Bob Study, Jami Sullivan-Dionisio, Darrin Tschopp, Sonny Tyler, Ron Warren, Dennis Watson, Robert Watson, Lael White, Alexis Wooley, and Dawn Worsham. Special thanks also to the cast and crew of "The Rare Breeds" Electronic Field Trip.

Further Readings

Alderson, Lawrence. *Rare Breeds,* 4th ed. Princes Risborough, England: Shire, 2001.

American Livestock Breeds Conservancy, http://albc-usa.org

Anderson, Virginia DeJohn. *Creatures of Empire: How Domestic Animals Transformed Early America.* New York: Oxford University Press, 2004.

Bowen, Joanne. "Foodways in the 18th-Century Chesapeake." In Theodore R. Reinhart, ed., *The Archaeology of 18th-Century Virginia.* Special Publication 35 of the Archaeological Society of Virginia. Richmond, VA: Spectrum Press, 1996.

Brown, Katharine L., and Nancy T. Sorrells. *Virginia's Cattle Story: The First Four Centuries.* Staunton, VA: Lot's Wife Publishing, 2004.

Carson, Jane. *Colonial Virginia Cookery: Procedures, Equipment, and Ingredients in Colonial Cooking.* Williamsburg, VA: The Colonial Williamsburg Foundation, 1985.

Carson, Jane. *Colonial Virginians at Play.* Williamsburg, VA: The Colonial Williamsburg Foundation, 1989.

Dohner, Janet Vorwald. *The Encyclopedia of Historic and Endangered Livestock and Poultry Breeds.* New Haven, CT: Yale University Press, 2001.

Hendricks, Bonnie L. *International Encyclopedia of Horse Breeds.* Norman, OK: University of Oklahoma Press, 1995.

Pawson, H. Cecil. *Robert Bakewell: Pioneer Livestock Breeder.* London: Crosby Lockwood & Son, 1957.

Stanley, Pat. *Robert Bakewell and the Longhorn Breed of Cattle.* Ipswich, England: Farming Press, 1995.

Voltz, Jeanne, and Elaine J. Harvell. *The Country Ham Book.* Chapel Hill, NC: University of North Carolina Press, 1999.